Rubiks Cube Solution For Kids

A Simple 7 Step Beginners Guide To Solving The Rubik's Cube Puzzle With Logic

Jayden Burns

Copyright © 2019 Jayden Burns

All rights reserved. No part of this publication may be reproduced, distributed or transmitted in any form or by any means, including photocopying, recording, or other electronic or mechanical methods, without the prior written permission of the publisher, except in the case of brief quotations embodied in critical reviews and certain other non-commercial uses permitted by copyright law.

Trademarked names appear throughout this book. Rather than use a trademark symbol with every occurrence of a trademarked name, names are used in an editorial fashion, with no intention of infringement of the respective owner's trademark. The information in this book is distributed on an "as is" basis, without warranty. Although every precaution has been taken in the preparation of this work, neither the author nor the publisher shall have any liability to any person or entity with respect to any loss or damage caused or alleged to be caused directly or indirectly by the information contained in this book.

Table Of Contents

Intro	4
Rubik's Cube Terminology	5
Cubies	6
Turns	8
Rotations	11
Rotation Examples	15
Double Turns	18
Practice Algorithms	19
Step One - Solving The Cross	22
Step Two - Solving The First Layer	33
Step Three - Solving The Middle Layer	36
Step Four - Making The Yellow Cross	39
Step Five - Completing The Yellow Face	41
Step Six - The Final Corners	44
Step Seven - Finishing The Cube	48
Benefits To Solving The Cube	52
Rubik's Cube Random Facts!	54
The History Of The Cube	61

Intro

Welcome to the fascinating world of Rubik's Cube! This little puzzle has dazzled people from all around the world for decades now, including its own founder Ezro Rubik, who took three months to complete his own invention.

Don't stress though. We're going to solve it in a fraction of that time with this simple step by step guide. After following this guide, you're going to have found all the answers you were after and will be rewarded with a perfectly solved cube just like you bought!

Before we begin and get into it, we need to learn a little terminology of the cube, which will make the process of solving the cube much easier!

Rubik's Cube Terminology

You probably have the cube sitting right next to you. If you don't, go grab it. Each side you see contains 9 cubes measuring 2.2 inches and is called a face. There are 6 faces on each Rubik's Cube with 6 different colors.

The original colors are white, yellow, blue, green, orange and red. With so many different Cubes in shops these days, yours might look a little different. Don't worry if yours is different though; the method will still work! Just match the color shown in the book to the one you have on your cube, and you'll be fine.

Each color on the cube is linked to another, just like each number on one side of a die is linked to a number on the other side where both add up to 7 (5 and 2, 6 and 1, 3 and 4). White will be opposite to yellow, green will be opposite to blue, and red will be opposite to orange.

We will follow this pattern in the rest of the book, so if your colors are a little different, make a note so you don't get lost!

Cubies

When you look on each face, you'll see the smaller separate cubes. These are called cubies. There are 26 separate cubies in the Rubik's Cube. You might think there are 27 because there are 9 on each face; however, there is no cubie in the very centre of the Rubik's cube, hence the 26. There are 3 different types of cubies on the cube:

Centre Cubie
There is a total of six centre cubies in the middle of each face. These pieces remain where they are and never move, as they're attached, as you'll see if you've ever taken one apart. With this information, we can conclude the color of each face will be the same as the color of each centre cubie; i.e., the centre cubie that is white means the whole face will be white once the cube is complete.

Edge Cubie
In total, there are twelve edge cubies with two colors on each. If we imagine a solved cube and are looking at the white side, we

will see a white/red piece, white/blue, white/green and a white/orange piece. There will never be a white/yellow piece, as they're on opposite sides of each other.

Corner Cubie

There are eight corner cubies in total, which have three colors on each cubie. If we imagine the solved cube again and we're looking at the white side, the corner cubies will be colored white/red/blue, white/red/green, white/green/orange, and white/orange/blue. Again, there will never be a white/yellow/blue piece, as white and yellow are on opposite sides of each other.

Turns

We're going to learn some terms for the sides of the cube, which will make the algorithms easier to follow in the next steps.

1. When looking at the cube, the face you're looking at will be known as 'front' or **F.**
2. The side opposite to it, or the one on the back, will be known as 'back' or **B.**
3. The side on the top, facing the roof will be known as us 'up' or **U.**
4. The side opposite the ceiling, facing the ground, will be known as 'down' or **D.**
5. The face on the 'left' will be known as **L.**
6. The face on the 'right' will be known as **R.**

From now on, we will begin using these terms, so quickly go through them a few times to familiarise yourself with them! If you're more of a visual person, there are some images below to help you better understand this.

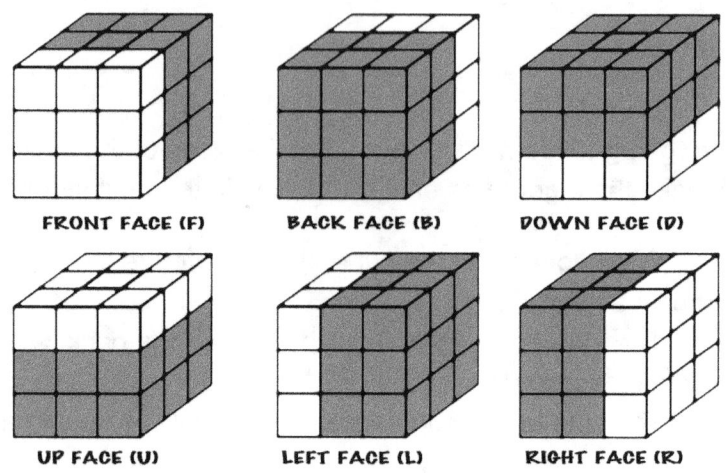

Throughout most of the book, we will be holding the cube in front of us like the image below:

Only in later steps we will be holding the cube facing another way, which will look like the image below:

Rotations

Now that we've learned all the sides, we're going to learn the rotations. This step is easy because we use what we've already learned! So, we have 6 sides, **F, B, L, R, D,** and **U**, which can be rotated either clockwise or anticlockwise.

The rotation for a clockwise turn is simply the letter, and for an anticlockwise rotation, there will be an 'i' after the letter ('i' stands for inverted).

There are some images below to help you visualise this.

Clockwise rotations

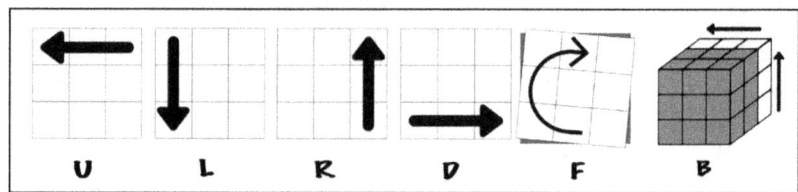

Anti-clockwise rotations

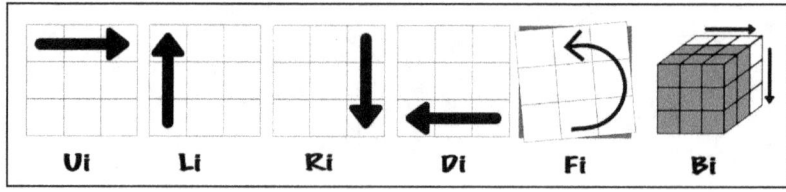

Important note: The rotations are clockwise and anti-clockwise in relation to their own face and not the face to which you're applying the algorithm. For example if we take the **Di** rotation:

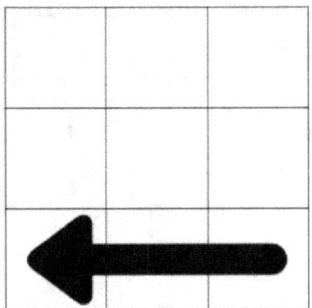

It looks like, when we do this rotation, it's going in a clockwise manner:

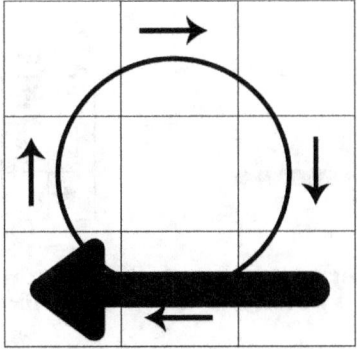

This is because we're looking at the face in front of us, and it's where we're going to apply the algorithm.

However, if we were looking at the bottom face directly, we see it is actually going in an anti-clockwise rotation:

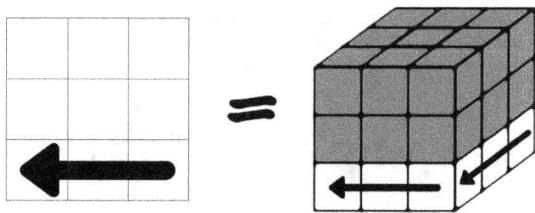

If you were looking at the bottom of the cube, the rotation would look like this:

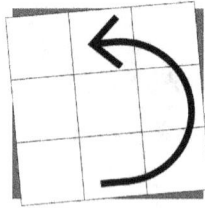

I.e., the face is actually rotating in an anti-clockwise rotation.

If this was a little confusing, stick to the images and rotate the cube just like the images and you'll be golden.

Rotation Examples

Let's practice a few times so we get the hang of seeing the letter and making our hands move to match what we see.

1. If we're looking at the cube and we see an **R**, this would mean we would turn the face
    on the right side clockwise, and we would see the three cubies on the front face move up.

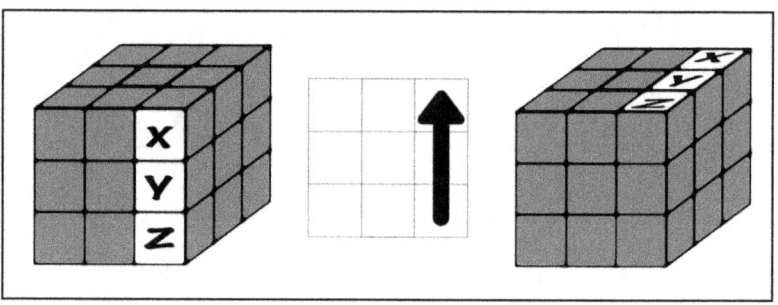

2. If we see a **D**, we would turn the face on the bottom facing the ground clockwise, and
    we would see the three cubies on the bottom layer move to the right.

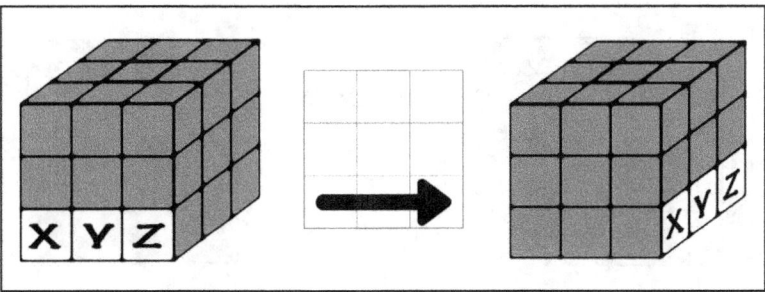

3.   If we see a **Li,** you would move the face on the left anti-clockwise, and you would see the three cubies on the left of the front face move up.

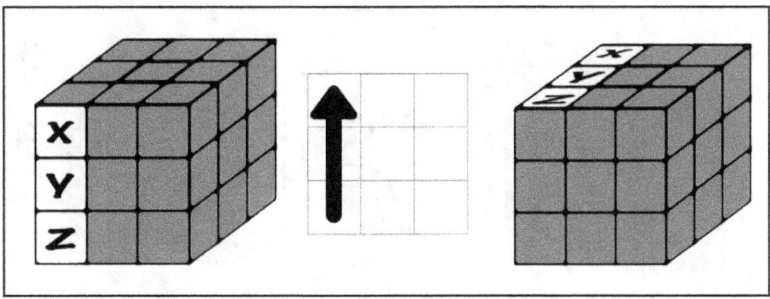

4.   If you see **Ui**, you would turn the face facing the ceiling anti-clockwise and you would
        see the three cubies of the front face turn to the right.

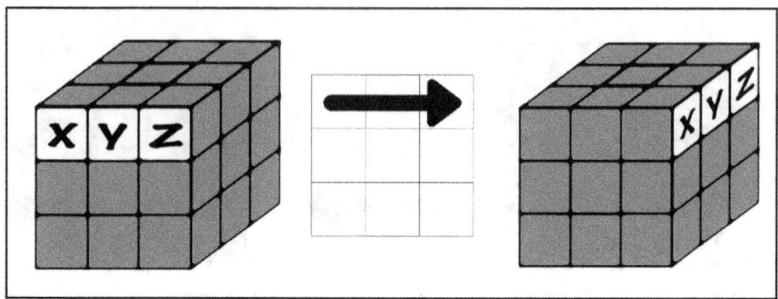

5. When you see **B** (or **Bi**), you won't notice any change in the front cubies, as this turn
only affects the face on the back.

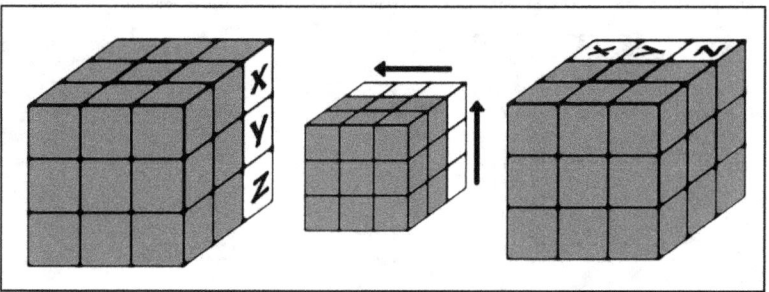

These examples should have helped you understand the turns of the cube a little better! In the following steps, we're going to be seeing a string of these letters, which are known as algorithms.

Double Turns

Before we move onto longer algorithms, let's have a quick look at double turns. This is simply when we want to turn a face 180 degrees. You will see, for example, **F F, D D, Ri Ri,** etc. To visualise this, let's imagine when we do the the **F F** turn. The cubie on the bottom right will now be on the top left.

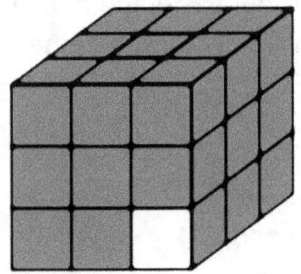 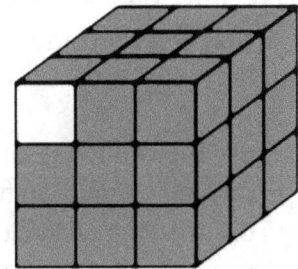

There is no difference whether you choose to turn the face clockwise or anti-clockwise twice, as you will get to the same place, so it's up to personal preference which way you decide to rotate it.

You will never see a triple rotation, as we can simply rotate the cube once the other way instead.

Practice Algorithms

We're going to go through a few practice drills, so we can begin to start turning the cube without having to think about it too much. This will be more beneficial, and you'll get more out of the exercise if you get a pen and paper and write it down as we go along.

We will go through the first one together to get the hang of things. If you were to read the following, what would the formula look like:

1.	Turn the right side once.
2.	Turn the down side twice.
3.	Turn the front anti clockwise once.
4.	Turn the left side once.

The algorithm would be: **R, D D, Fi, L**

Have a go by yourself and see how you do! Good luck.

1.	Turn the left side twice, the up side anti-clockwise once, the back side twice, the down side twice, and the front side anti-clockwise once.
2.	Turn the back side twice, the front side twice, the left side anti-clockwise once, the right side once, and the down side once.

3. Turn the up side anti-clockwise once, the down side once, the right side anti-clockwise twice, and the front anti-clockwise twice.

Turn to the next page to see the answers.

Answers

Did you get the following?

1. **L L, Ui, B B, D D, Fi**
2. **B B, F F, Li, R, D**
3. **Ui, D, Ri Ri, Fi Fi** (For the last two, you would have gotten the same result if you did **R R** or **F F** for the last two rotations).

If you got these, congratulations! You're ready to move onto the first stage of solving the Cube. If you didn't, go back and have another go.

Step One - Solving The Cross

If your Cube is still intact, now is the time to jumble it up! Don't worry. It'll be looking as good as new in no time. We will concentrate on solving the white side first and suggest you do the same color, as it'll be easier to follow along.

The goal for this step, as seen in the image above, is to create a white cross as well as having the edge cubies of the white cross align with the color of the centre cubie on the other side. A lot of this is done with some trial and error and some practice, but there are some tips!

    a. The first step is going to be to find the white centre cubie and bring it up, so it's facing the top/ceiling.

b. The second step is going to be finding an edge cubie with white on it. Let's look for the white/blue edge cubie and put that in place. Once you've found where it is, move to the next step. (The image below is what we're trying to do to give you an idea.)

c. There may be a few different spots where the white/blue edge cubie will be. We want to get it so it's on the face with the blue centre cubie, so we can apply an algorithm. If your cube looks like one of the images below, move onto step **d** and apply the algorithm.

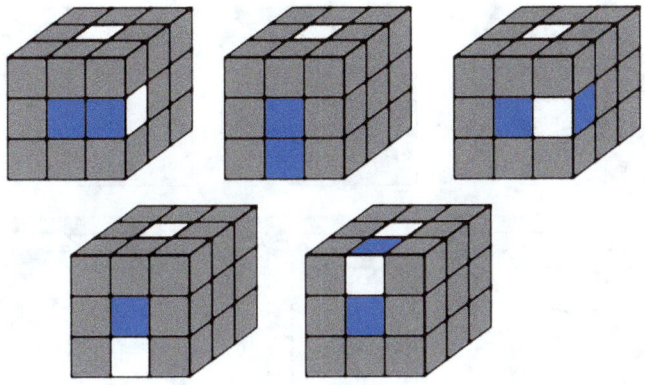

If your cubie is not there, it will be in one of the following spots:

- Your cubie is on the up layer: Rotate the **U** layer until it is with the blue centre cubie.

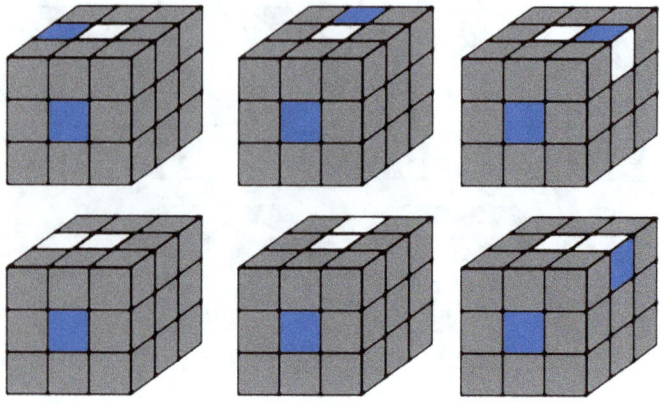

Rotate the **U** layer 1-3 times to get it to where we want it, just like the image below.

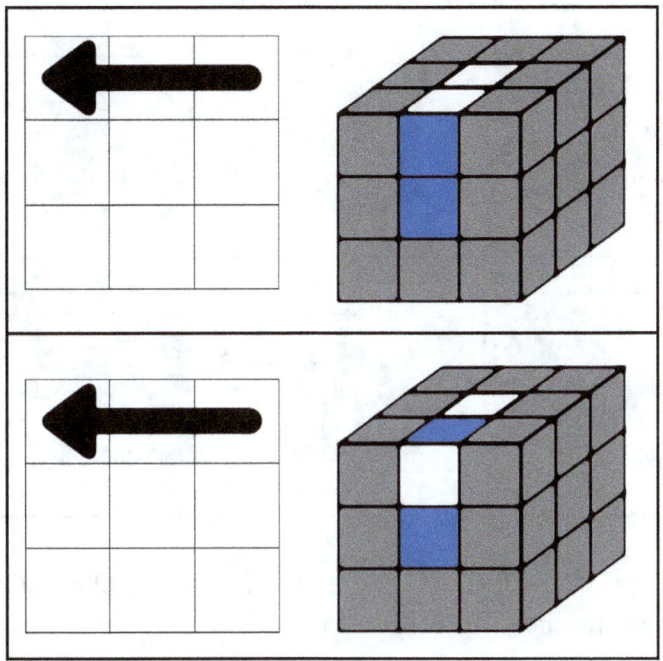

- Your cubie is on the middle layer: Rotate the layer where the blue/white edge cubie is to face the top then rotate towards the blue centre cubie

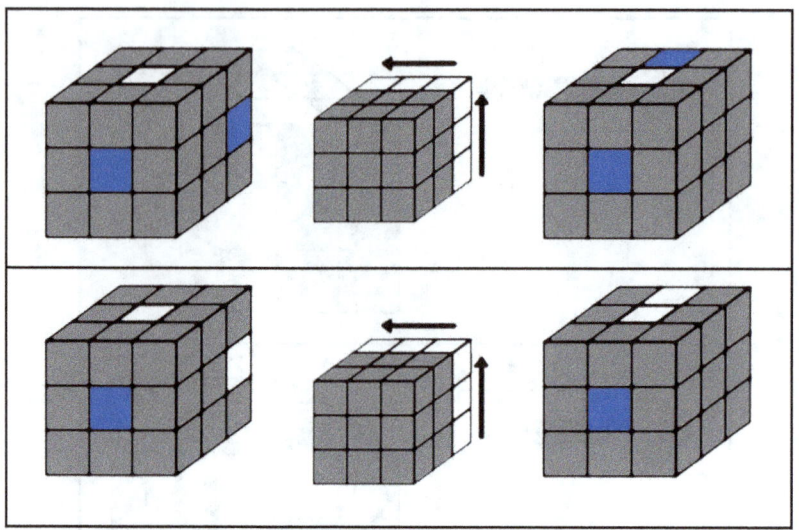

Once here, rotate the **U** 1-3 times to get it to the blue face as we did for the previous step.

- Your cubie is on the bottom layer: Rotate the **D** layer 1-3 times until it is with the blue centre cubie.

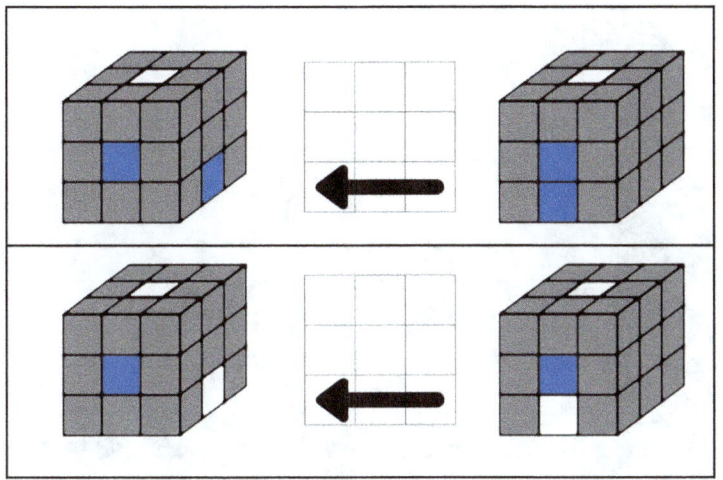

d. Now your cube should look like one of the following images. Apply the formula and we'll have the white/blue edge cubie exactly where we want it.

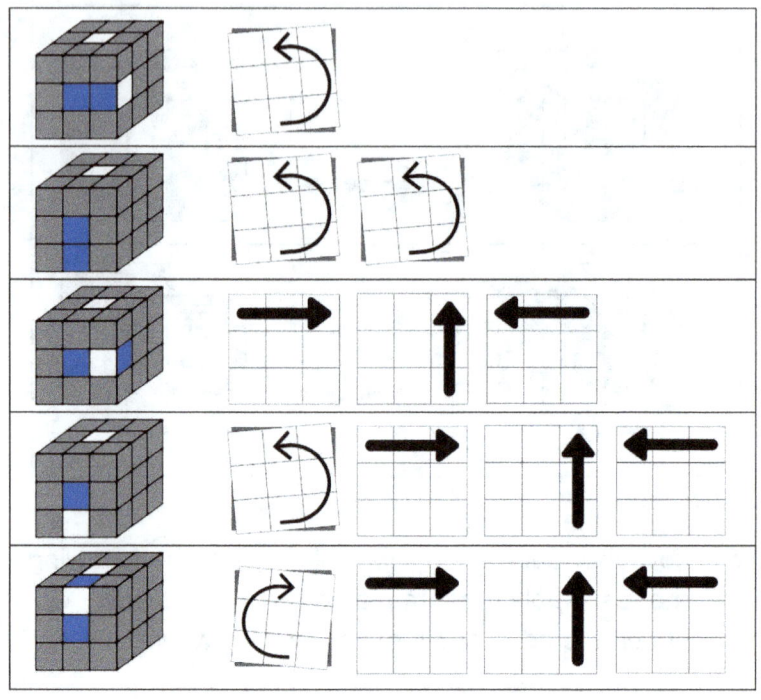

(Fi)
(Fi Fi)
(Ui R U)
(Fi Ui R U)
(F Ui R U)

Your blue/white cubie should now be in place like the image below!

This step is intuitive and takes a little practice. Use the above algorithms to complete the rest of the cross without messing up the sides you've already done.

We will go over a few more examples below if needed. These are just a few and don't cover all the scenarios; however, your cube will be a variation of one of the below.

Let's put the white/orange piece where it needs to go after we have the white blue/edge cubie where it needs to be.

Example 1a:

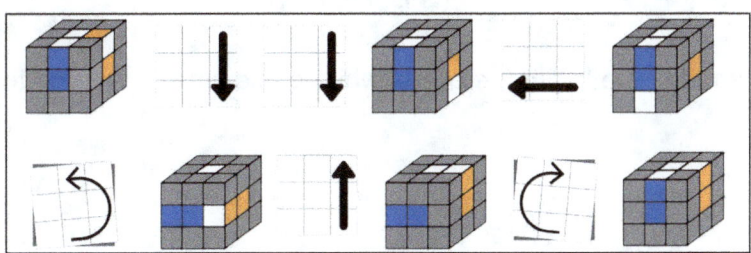

(R R, Di, Fi, R, F)

Example 1b:

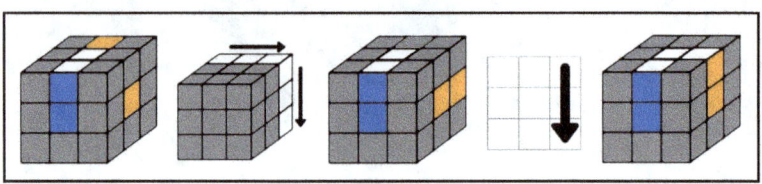

(Bi, Ri)

Example 1c:

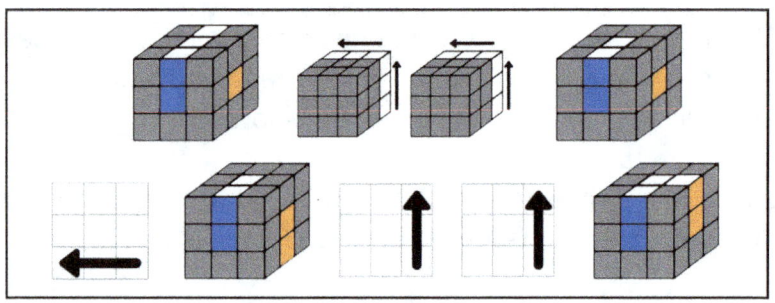

(B B, Di, R R)

Example 2, let's put the green/white cubie where it needs to go.

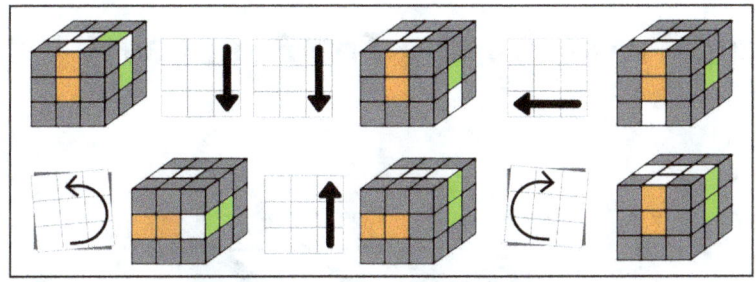

(Ri Ri, Di, Fi, R, F)

Example 3, let's put the white/red cubie where it needs to go.

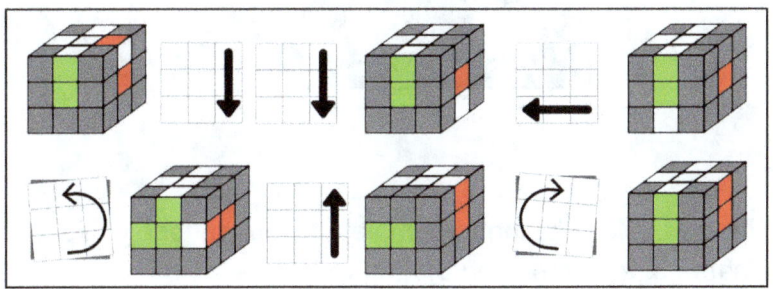

(Ri Ri, Di, Fi, R, F)

Step Two - Solving The First Layer

In this step, we're going to complete the white face while, at the same time completing the top row.

Continue holding the cube so the white face cross is facing the top. Find a corner cubie that has the color white on it. Let's look for the white/blue/red corner cubie and complete that one. If it's already complete, lucky you! If not, apply the algorithm below.

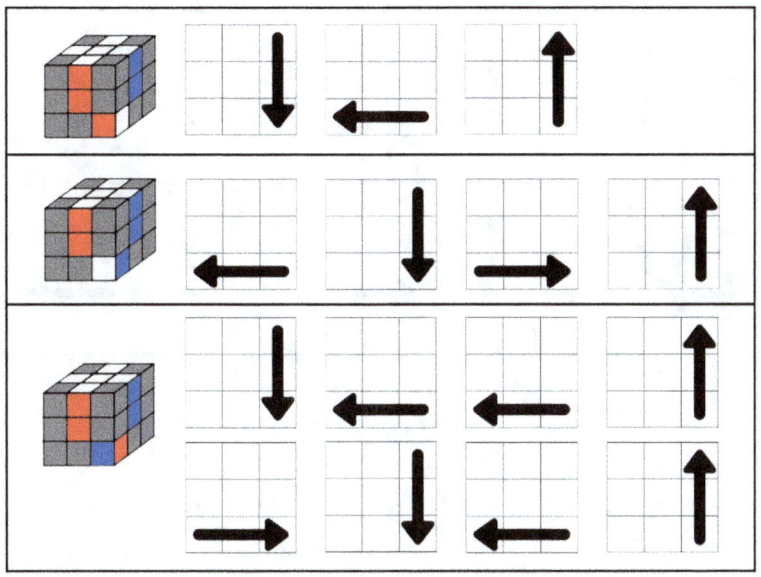

(Ri, Di, R)
(Di, Ri, D, R)
(Ri, Di Di, R, D, Ri, Di, R)

Note: Your cubie may already be in its spot but not in the right way. If that's the case, apply the algorithm below, which will put it to where we want it and we can then apply the formula above.

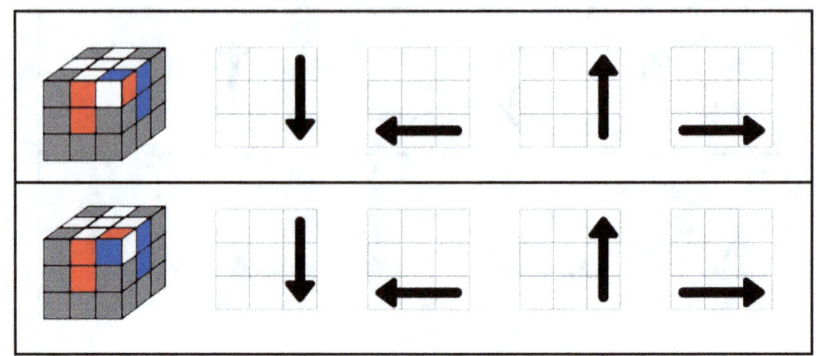

(Ri, Di, R, D)

Step Three - Solving The Middle Layer

The next step to completing the cube is to solve the middle layer so that it looks like the image above.

Let's continue with the blue face and find the blue/red cubie, so we can apply the formula. Again, there might be a few possible solutions where this edge cubie might be. It might already be in the spot we want it to be, which is great! You can apply the same algorithm to another color of the cube. It might be on the bottom layer, which is where we want it or it could be in its spot but inverted. Either way, we only need to learn 2 formulas to complete this step.

If the cube is in its spot but inverted, let's get it out of there and onto the bottom layer. While looking at the red face, apply the formula below.

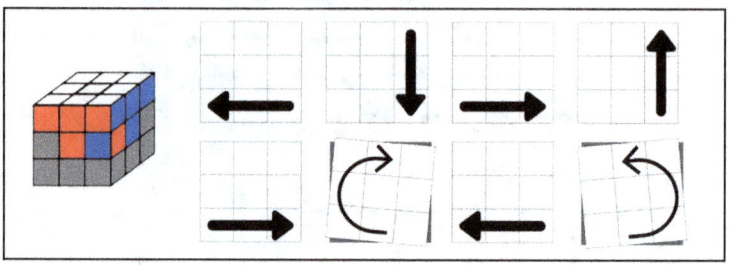

(Di, Ri, D, R, D, F, Di, Fi)

The blue/red cubie will now be on the bottom layer. Rotate it so it is matching with its centre cubie as shown below and then apply the algorithm again.

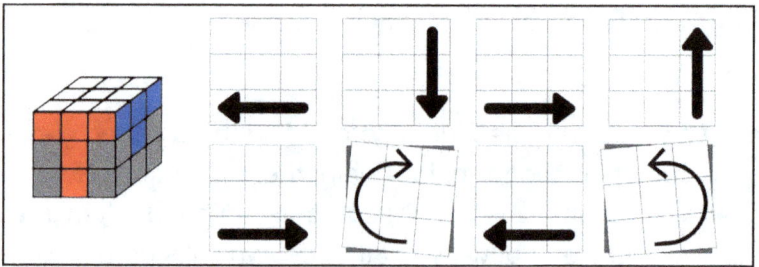

(Di, Ri, D, R, D, F, Di, Fi)

If the blue cubie is in front of you, we want to send it to the left between the red and the blue centre cubies, so let's apply the following algorithm. Make sure you're facing the **blue** face.

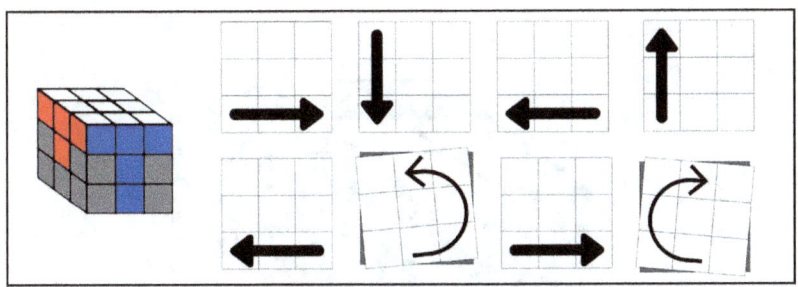

(D, L, Di, Li, Di, Fi, D, F)

Note: A quick tip is to complete the color that already has the edge cubie on the bottom layer. It will be much quicker than popping the edge cubie out of a wrong spot to put on the bottom layer and then applying the algorithm again to put it back into place. By putting the edge cubies into the right spot, it will pop out any edge cubies from the incorrect spot.

We can now apply the same formula to the rest of the edge cubies by following the same concept as above. Get the edge cubie matching the centre cubie and apply the first algorithm if you want it to go to the right and the second algorithm if you want it to go to the left.

Step Four - Making The Yellow Cross

Now that the white face and the two bottom layers are complete, we're going to complete the yellow cross. We can turn the cube over, so the white is on the bottom and the yellow centre cubie is facing the top. This is how we'll hold the cube now until we complete it.

There will be a few ways that the yellow face looks like after you complete the first two layers. You may be lucky and already see the cross, in which case you can move onto 'Step Five - Completing The Yellow Face'. Otherwise, your cube will look like the following. Apply the following algorithm until you get the cross. You don't need to be facing any particular way as long as the yellow is on the top.

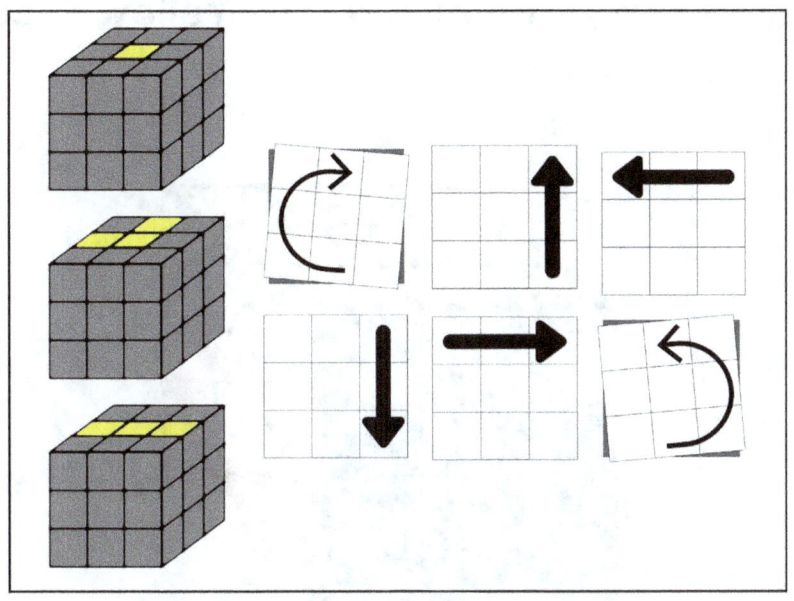

(F R U Ri Ui Fi)

(Apply the formula 1-3 times to get the cross)

Note: You may see a variation of the above 3 patterns with some extra yellow cubies on the face.

Step Five - Completing The Yellow Face

We're now going to complete the yellow face by getting the yellow corner cubies facing the top. They're not going to be exactly where they need to go, but we're going to solve that in the next step.

Similar to the previous step, there are going to be a few different ways that the cube might look. Your cubie will look like either of the bottom few images. Find the face your cube looks like and apply the algorithm.

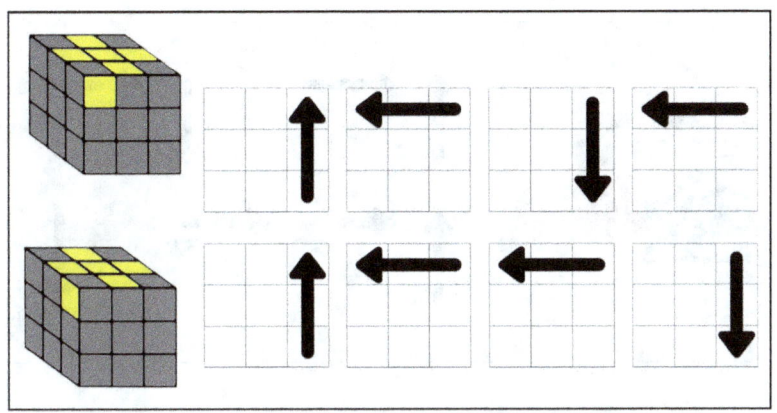

(R, U, Ri, U, R, U, U, Ri)

If yours looks like the above, apply the algorithm 1-3 times until it looks like one of the below images and then apply the required formula.

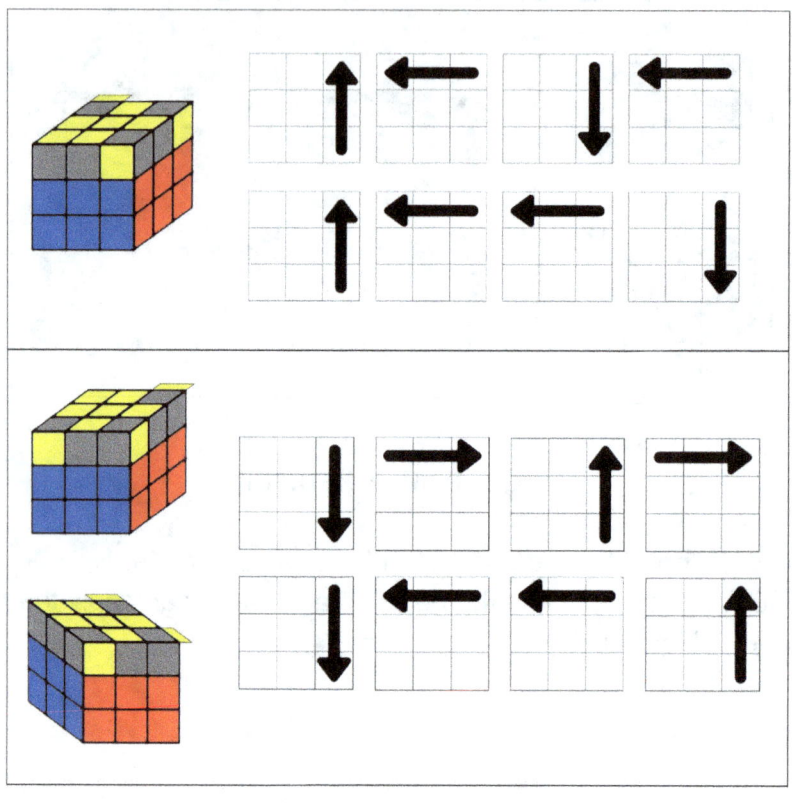

(R, U, Ri, U, R, U, U, Ri)
(Ri, Ui, R, Ui, Ri, Ui, Ui, R)

Note: If you've done this algorithm more than once and haven't completed the yellow side, it may be because you were holding the cube the wrong way. Try again, facing the correct way, and the yellow side will be completed!

Step Six - The Final Corners

We're now going to switch the corner cubies in place, so they match their respective faces like the image above.

There are three possible patterns you will see on your cube:

a. You may have gotten lucky and your cube already has the corner cubies in the right spot like the image above. You can move onto 'Step Seven'.

b. Your cube may have two correct corner cubies in the right position diagonally from one another, but the other two are incorrect. For example, the yellow/red/blue cubie and the yellow/orange/green cubie are exactly where they need to be.

c. Your cube will have two correct corner cubies on the same face. This will mean one face is almost complete, except for the centre top cubie. As the image below shows, the yellow/blue/red and the yellow/blue/green cubie are exactly where they need to be.

If your cube looks like **b**, apply the formula below. It doesn't matter which face you're looking at as long as white is on the bottom and yellow is on the top.

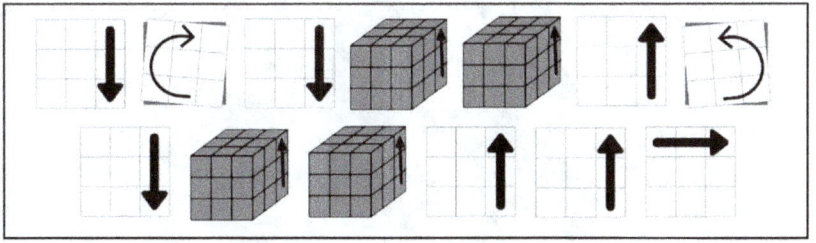

(Ri, F, Ri, B B, R, Fi, Ri, B B, R R, Ui)

If your cube looks like number 3, put the face that is almost complete (the red face) so it's facing the back and apply the algorithm below:

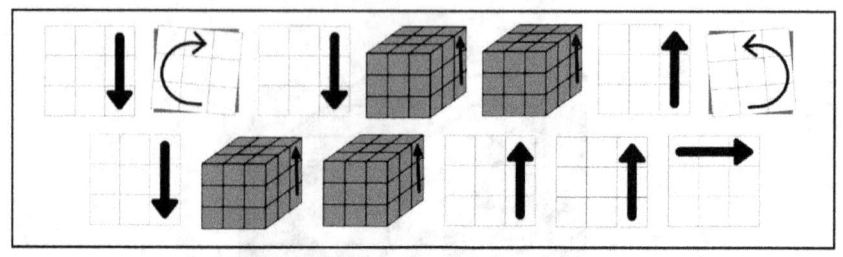

(Ri, F, Ri, B, B, R, Fi, Ri, B B, R R, Ui)

Step Seven - Finishing The Cube

There are three patterns your cube might look like.

a. Your cube may be solved! This doesn't happen often, but if it did, congratulations!

b. All four of the top centre cubies may be out of place.

c. Only three of the four top centre cubies may be out of place.

If yours looks like **b**, apply the algorithm below facing any face as long as white is on the bottom and yellow is on the top.

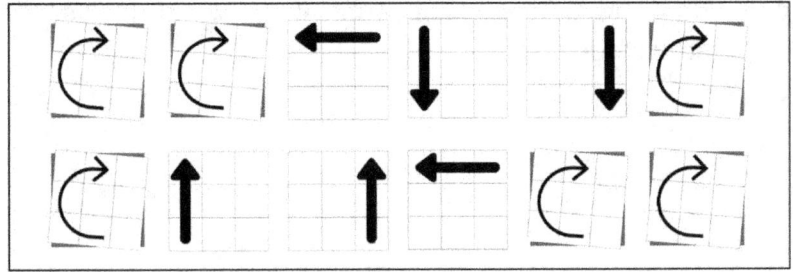

(F F, U, L, Ri, F F, Li, R, U, F F)

It should now look like **c**.

If yours looks like **c**, face the complete side on the **B** and apply the formula:

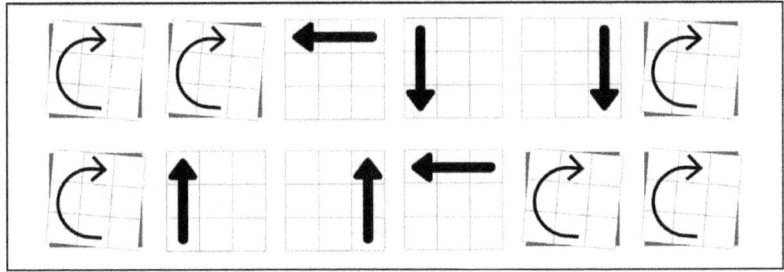

(F F, U, L, Ri, F F, Li, R, U, F F)

You may have to complete this formula twice or three times to solve the cube completely.

CONGRATULATIONS!! Your cube should now be complete. You've now entered the 1% of people in the world who've competed the cube.

Benefits To Solving The Cube

Did you know there are many benefits to solving the cube? It's not just a cool party trick and there are benefits to solving it continuously, even after you've completed it once. They include both mental and physical benefits!

The mental benefits include:

1. Your ability to reframe a problem. You'll be able to see in new perspectives on how to solve problems, possibly a birds-eye view in seeing solutions from another angle.
2. Better memory. When solving the cube, you have to learn algorithms and apply them in a sequential order, otherwise scrambling the cube. Recalling these algorithms from memory exercises the brain, keeping it fit and healthy.
3. Increased recall. Solving the cube will stimulate quicker thinking, which will translate to better recall in other aspects of your life.
4. Learning how to break complex tasks into small and simple steps.
5. An increase in concentration & attention to detail. With regular practice of the cube you'll improve your ability to resist external distractions and learn how to focus on what's right in front of you.
6. Becoming more efficient in problem solving & optimisation. The Rubik's cube is a complicated mathematical conundrum in the form of a toy. If you learn

to solve this, you'll have the ability to solve and work through other complex problems.
7. Mental fortitude. Solving the Rubik's Cube takes patience, commitment, and persistence. Once you've put in the time and effort necessary to solve it, you'll have confidence in other areas of your life when you come across similar puzzles or situations when you'll use your mind the same way.

The physical benefits include:

1.   Finger agility and dexterity
2.   Better reflexes the more you solve it
3.   Increased eye-hand coordination

Rubik's Cube Random Facts!

1. There are now Cubers who are able to solve the Cube blindfolded. In 2016, Chang Hong Lik, a seven-year-old cuber, successfully completed the cube blindfolded in a little over two minutes by memorising the location of all the squares before being blindfolded.
2. Over 350 million Cubes have been sold worldwide since its introduction, becoming the best-selling toy in history.
3. One of the most remarkable Rubik's Cube Facts is that a three-year-old girl from China solved the Cube in 114 seconds, becoming the youngest person ever to solve it!
4. There are 43 quintillion possible ways a Rubik's cube can be reordered, meaning 43 with 18 zeros after it. The small 2x2 Pocket Cube has over three million rearrangement ways, while the 7x7 has a one-hundred-and-sixty-digit number.
5. A new art movement, known as Rubik's Cubism, was born, consisting of using solved cubes to create a mosaic effect. In 2009, the artist Josh Chalom re-created 'Last Supper' by Da Vinci using over 4000 Cubes and, later, the 'Hand Of God' by Michelangelo using over 12,000 Cubes. This last one measured 29 feet by 15 feet and weighed over a ton. The artist confessed to having bought one dollar cubes from China to save money.
6. Some cubers began to find the Rubik's cube too easy, which has led to some new cube variations. Some

examples of these are the cube with faces instead of colors, the Sudoku Cube, the Shepherd's Cube with black and white arrows, the Maze Cube and, my favorite one, the Braille Cube with tactile stickers for blind people to solve the cube.

7. In 2010, a team of researchers found out that any randomly scrambled cube can be solved in 20 moves or less. This gave rise to the idea that God's number is 20, meaning that, if God was to do a mixed up cube, it would take him 20 moves to do it without cheating. This magic number became one of the biggest secrets in the Rubik's Cube community that took 30 years to find. The notion of God's number was discovered in 1981, when researchers thought the number was somewhere between 18 and 52; thirty-five years later, the idea was proved by Google's supercomputers. So far, no human has yet figured out God's number, nor have they implemented it.

8. In 1982, the cube had to be modified in order to enter the England sales market. Health officials found there were unsafe levels of lead in the squares of the cube. They contained at least 26,250 ppm (parts per million) of lead compared to the 2500 ppm allowed.

9. Since the cube's creation, sales have remained constant. In 2006, however, there was a huge increase in sales thanks to the movie 'The Pursuit of Happiness' featuring Will Smith. In the trailer, Will's character is shown solving a cube, which ignited the passion of a new generation of cubers 27 years later.

10. The largest Rubik's cube in the world is 5 feet long and 5 feet tall (1.5 x 1.5 meters). Despite its size and weight, 220 pounds or 100 kilograms, it is 100%

functional and moves in all ways. On the contrary, the smallest Cube measures just 6mm currently, with people trying to create an even smaller one!

11. You would need 1,400 trillion years to perform all possible arrangements of the cube if you turned one cube per second. In other words, if you started this project from when the big bang happened, you still wouldn't be done yet.
12. The 'Devil's Number' is another term used to refer to the smallest number of moves required to visit every possible mixed version of the cube. This number has been more difficult to find. The number has not even been found for the 2x2 cube.
13. There is a cube that was created that is 33 by 33 by 33, making it the most complex cube ever created. You would need 1,666 regular cubes to equally reach the numbers as this one. This cube holds a World Record and is 100% legitimate. Each layer can be rotated 180 degrees, creating a checkerboard pattern, which is the requirement to get into the Guinness Book Of Records. You can see the layers rotating on YouTube. 205 hours of work, 6534 stickers, and 6153 3D printed parts were needed to create this cube. Each layer is 4.1mm thick. If you thought the regular cube's 43 times 10 to the power of 18 (43×10^{18}) combinations were impressive, this cube has 1.159 times 10 to the power of 4094 (1.159×10^{4094}) possibilities.
14. There is a record out there that includes a person solving the cube using only their feet in just 20.57 seconds.
15. In 1995, Fred Cueller, founder and CEO of Diamond Cutters International, designed the Masterpiece Cube

to celebrate the 15th anniversary of the Rubik's Cube. The cube was made with over 185-carats of different gemstones in replacement of the bright stickers, such as 18 carats of yellow gold, 34 carats of rubies, 34 carats of emeralds, and 22.5 carats of amethyst. The violet color of the amethyst replaced the orange side to avoid copycats replicating the Masterpiece creation. This fully functional and stunning cube took around 8500 hours of work to be created.

16. In 2015, Keven Hays from the United States joined the book of records by solving 8 cubes under water in a single breath. This record might be broken someday; meanwhile, don't hold your breath over it.
17. 'Cubaholics' is the term used among the Cubing world for people who experience compulsive behavior towards the cube. This includes feeling pain in the wrist and thumb, known as Rubik's Wrist and Cuber's Thumb, respectively. In 1982, the 'Cubaholics Anonymous' group was created.
18. Computer nerds fascinated by the Rubik's cube invented a robot capable of solving the cube in .38 seconds. This includes scanning, processing, and completion of all rotations.
19. Another impressive feat achieved by Que Jianyu, a thirteen-year-old boy from China, placed him in the Guinness Book of Records. Que solved three Rubik's cubes in the fastest time possible while juggling them, becoming the first person to do so. After training for two years, Que achieved the feat live on stage during a Chinese TV show named iDream (the equivalent to America's Got Talent). Before doing the stunt, Que had 15 seconds to look at the three cubes. The three cubes

were constantly thrown up in the air; every time one landed in his right hand, he turned a side before throwing it right back up. The movements happened so fast that it was not even possible to see his fingers. Que completed the three cubes successfully in a matter of five minutes and six seconds.

20. There are several events that take place during the World Championships of Cubing besides just solving the regular three by three cube. One of these events is known as the Multi-Blind, where the mission is to complete as many Rubik's Cubes as possible in an hour while being blindfolded. 48 solved cubes is the current record held by Shivam Bansal, who took 36 minutes to memorize the scrambled cubes and used the remaining 24 minutes to solve them all.
21. The first episode of 'Rubik, the Amazing Cube' was aired in 1983 by ABC. Although having no narrative at all, a 13-episode animated season was made.
22. Yusheng Du managed to complete the cube in less than a breath. With an impressive 3.47, he beat the preceding 4.22-second record achieved by 22-year-old Australian Feliks Zemdegs, becoming the fastest cuber in the world. The record still awaits to be broken, if possible...
23. Speedcubers prefer not to use Rubik's branded cubes. They blame the original patent holder for trying to monopolize the industry, rather than making better cubes that can compete with other brands, as they intimidate and abuse intellectual property law. In an attempt to bridge the gap in the cubing community, Red Bull and the Rubik's Brand recently partnered to

organize a World Championship, where only Rubik's branded cubes are to be used by all competitors.

24. Based on Rubiks.com statistics, one in seven people have tried to solve the Cube. This means one billion people! However, only 4% of the world's population can successfully solve a Rubik's cube. If solving it under a minute, then it represents 1% of total world.

25. In 1981, Patrick Bosset, a 13-year-old cuber, created the book 'You Can Do The Cube', which accidentally became a New York Times best seller. New and quicker methods to solve the puzzle were in high demand by cubers in the 80's, and this book was what everyone was looking for. The book was initially intended for his friends; however, one of the friends showed it to his father, who turned out to be an editor at Penguin Books. It's gone on to sell over 750,000 copies.

26. Joining the record books for this little puzzle is a hard feat these days, as so many records have been made throughout the years. In 2003, Dan Knight accomplished an impressive feat by jumping out of a plane and solving the cube while he fell. Jumping from 12,000 feet gave him 45 seconds of free fall before he had to deploy his parachute. He was able to complete the cube in 32 seconds. The cube was attached by drilling a hole in it and looping it to his wrist to prevent falling.

27. Yusheng Du managed to complete the cube in less than a breath. With an impressive 3.47, he beat the preceding 4.22 second record achieved by 22-year-old Australian Feliks Zemdegs, becoming the fastest cuber

in the world. The record still awaits to be broken, if possible...

The History Of The Cube

1974

- Erno Rubik, a Hungarian architect, created the first 3x3 prototype version of the Cube, as he wanted to have a working model that would help him better understand three-dimensional geometry. Its dimensions were larger than the standard size of the current cubes and was made out of wood.
- After creating the 'magical cube', as he called it, it turned out that he couldn't solve it himself. The more rotations he made, the more scrambled the cube got. As he wrote: "It was a code I myself had invented! Yet I could not read it."
- Three months later, he finally figured out how to solve his own invention.

1975

- The 'Magic Cube' was patented by Erno in Hungary. Five years later, the cube was re-named after himself.

1977

- Budapest was the place where the first batch of Cubes was launched. They were built in a way that couldn't be easily taken apart or broken, ideal as they were sold as children's toys.

1979

- The 'Iron Curtain' (a boundary dividing Europe into the former Soviet bloc and the West during communism) prevented the Cube from worldwide distribution for several years.

1980

- The Cube finally debuted internationally. It was slightly modified based on the rules and regulations concerning safety and packaging specificities established by the West. In this year, the name also changed from the 'Magic Cube' to the 'Rubik's Cube'.
- It was during this time when the first layer-by-layer method of how to complete the cube was published by David Singmaster, a retired professor of mathematics, puzzle lover, and passionate promoter of the Rubik's Cube. Many cubers today still use his method.

1981

- In 1980 and 1981, the Cube received the Toy of the Year Award, selling more than one hundred million units in the first three years.

1982

- The first Rubik's Cube World Championship was held in Budapest, Hungary. Twenty people from around the world were chosen to compete after winning previous competitions within their home countries.
- The American teenager Minh Thai was the first to win the Rubik's Cube World Championships, completing the cube in 22.95 seconds. After his victory, he published a book named *The Winning Solution,* teaching others how to solve the cube. The 'Ortega Corners-First' method used by many these days was later published based in this book.
- With the evolution of technology and computers over the next twenty years, the initial interest for this toy slowly diminished. The toy still remained on shelves in stores, however, weren't selling as they once did.

1995

- For the fifteen year anniversary of the cube, Diamond Cutters International designed a 'Masterpiece Cube' valued at $1.5 million, becoming the most expensive cube in the world.

1997

- A new method for solving the Cube was published by Jessica Fridrich; it was named after herself as the

Fridrich method. The method is considered one of the best and has been followed by most of the world record cubers, despite Jessica herself stating that she finds it to be an inefficient method.

2003

- Ron Van Bruchem and Tyson Mao created the World Cube Association (WCA), the first official organisation which aimed to run speedcubing competitions, as well as monitor national and international records. The organisation has also helped to spread the cube's passion to other countries around the globe, and it has now become the worldwide official speedcubing association. Potential new records must meet WCA rules and regulations to be accepted.

2005

- Special edition cube packaging was released for the 25th year celebration of the Cube.
- Jeans Pons won the third edition of the Worldwide Championships with a time of 15.10 seconds.

2014

- The 40th anniversary of the Rubik's Cube was celebrated since its creation in 1974. An interactive Rubik's Cube was deployed by Google on its front page.

- New Jersey was the location chosen for the 2014 US National Championships, as well as for the "Beyond Rubik's Cube" exhibition at the Liberty Science Centre. The exhibition gathered every possible thing related to the cube, including robots, solving algorithms, the original wood prototype, and even Rubik himself.
- Every two years, the Rubik's Cube Championships and the European Championships are held, on alternating years between them. Worldwide passionate cubers gather to compete and try to beat the previous year's world record. The current world record is held by Yusheng Du, as of 2018, with 3.47 seconds.

If you enjoyed this book and it helped you at all it would mean the world to me if you could leave a quick review. Join the top 1% of the world who've completed the cube and show off by taking a photo of yourself with the cube and uploading it with the review with the hashtag **#RubiksCubeChallenge**. Congratulations again and I look forward to seeing it!

www.ingramcontent.com/pod-product-compliance
Lightning Source LLC
Chambersburg PA
CBHW071034080526
44587CB00015B/2613